NAP LAJOIE
SECOND BASEMAN

CLEVELAND
INDIANS

MANNY RAMIREZ
RIGHT FIELDER

CLEVELAND
INDIANS

THE STORY OF THE CLEVELAND INDIANS

Published by Creative Education
P.O. Box 227, Mankato, Minnesota 56002
Creative Education is an imprint of The Creative Company
www.thecreativecompany.us

Design and production by Blue Design
Art direction by Rita Marshall
Printed by Corporate Graphics in the United States of America

Photographs by Getty Images (Victor Baldizon/MLB Photos, Al Bello, Jonathan Daniel/Allsport, Diamond Images, G Fiume, Otto Greule Jr, Harry How, Kidwiler Collection/Diamond Images, Nick Laham, Major League Baseball Photos/MLB Photos, MPI, National Baseball Hall of Fame Library/MLB Photos, Nivek Neslo, G Newman Lowrance, Photo File, Photo File/MLB Photos, Tom Pidgeon/Allsport, Rich Pilling/MLB Photos, Gregory Shamus, George Silk/Time & Life Pictures, Jared Wickerham), Bryan Hunter

Library of Congress Cataloging-in-Publication Data

LeBoutillier, Nate.
The story of the Cleveland Indians / by Nate LeBoutillier.
p. cm. — (Baseball: the great American game)
Includes index.
Summary: The history of the Cleveland Indians professional baseball team from its inaugural 1871 season to today, spotlighting the team's greatest players and most memorable moments.
ISBN 978-1-60818-038-7
1. Cleveland Indians (Baseball team)—History—Juvenile literature. I. Title. II. Series.

GV875.C7L43 2011
796.357'640977132—dc22   2010024395

CPSIA: 110310 PO1381

First Edition
9 8 7 6 5 4 3 2 1

Page 3: Shortstop Lou Boudreau
Page 4: Pitcher Fausto Carmona

THE STORY
OF THE
CLEVELAND
INDIANS

Nate LeBoutillier

CREATIVE EDUCATION

CONTENTS

AN EARLY BASEBALL HOTBED

In 1796, a group of pioneers from the Connecticut Land Company led by Moses Cleaveland—a politician, land surveyor, and former Civil War soldier—founded a settlement in Ohio that became known as Cleveland. The city grew slowly at first, but by the latter half of the 19th century, Cleveland was booming, thanks to its proximity to two notable waterways—the Cuyahoga River to the west and Lake Erie to the north. The manufacturing of iron and iron products became big business, and Cleveland's robust economy drew multitudes of immigrant workers, giving the city a lasting reputation as a diverse multicultural center.

The city of Cleveland is also home to the Indians, a franchise in Major League Baseball's American League (AL). The state of Ohio was one of the first real hotspots for professional baseball; it was there, in Cincinnati, that the very first pro franchise was formed in 1869. And although it wasn't until 1901 that the franchise that was to become

In the 1800s, Cleveland was nicknamed "The Forest City," reflecting its status as an important settlement in a region still largely untamed.

PITCHER · BOB FELLER

Bob Feller took the league by storm when he struck out 15 batters in his first major-league start on August 23, 1936, against the St. Louis Browns. "Rapid Robert" had a scorching fastball that was the standard to which all pitchers after him were held. The right-hander went on to play the rest of his career with the Indians, winning 20 or more games in a season 6 times, capturing 7 AL strikeout titles, and leading the league 4 times in shutouts. Even though Feller's service in the U.S. Navy during World War II interrupted his baseball career, he remains the winningest pitcher in Cleveland's history.

BOB FELLER
PITCHER

CLEVELAND
INDIANS

STATS

Indians seasons: 1936–41, 1945–56

Height: 6 feet

Weight: 185

- 266–162 career record

- 1940 AL leader in wins, ERA, and strikeouts

- 8-time All-Star

- Baseball Hall of Fame inductee (1962)

known as the Indians became a permanent part of Cleveland, by then the city already had a well-established tradition of the game of summer.

It was 1871 when a team called the Cleveland Forest Citys began play as a member of one of the first pro baseball leagues, the National Association. In 1889, another club named the Cleveland Spiders fielded a team in the National League (NL). In 1890, the Spiders featured pitcher Cy Young, a native of the nearby city of Gilmore, Ohio. Young pitched for the club for 9 seasons, racking up 241 of his eventual 511 victories—a career tally that remains the major-league record. The Spiders folded after the 1899 season, when they finished an embarrassing 20–134.

Before that team disappeared, though, another Spiders player not named Young left his mark on Cleveland baseball history. American Indian outfielder Louis "Chief" Sockalexis earned renown for his fleet feet and cannon throwing arm before an ankle injury ended his career at a mere three seasons. Hall of Fame shortstop and manager Hughie Jennings, who played against Sockalexis as a member of the Baltimore Orioles, said, "At no time has a player crowded so many remarkable accomplishments into such a short period of time as Sockalexis." During

Sockalexis's days, sportswriters occasionally referred to Cleveland's team as "the Indians," a name that would later become official.

In 1901, the Cleveland Blues joined seven other charter franchises in forming the AL. In 1902, second baseman Napoleon "Nap" Lajoie and pitcher Addie Joss suited up for Cleveland's team, which became known as the Bronchos. Joss befuddled hitters with his big windup delivery, but it was Lajoie who would prove to be an especially vital acquisition to the development of Cleveland's franchise.

Lajoie became known for his remarkable all-around skill. "Every play he made was executed so gracefully that it looked like it was the easiest thing in the world," said Pittsburgh Pirates infielder Tommy Leach. Cleveland thought so highly of Lajoie that the franchise changed its name to the "Naps" in 1903 and made Lajoie player/manager in 1905. Cleveland was ready to start winning.

Star hurler Addie Joss supplemented his income—and planned for life after baseball—by taking up sports writing during the off-season. Sadly, he would die at 31.

ADDIE JOSS

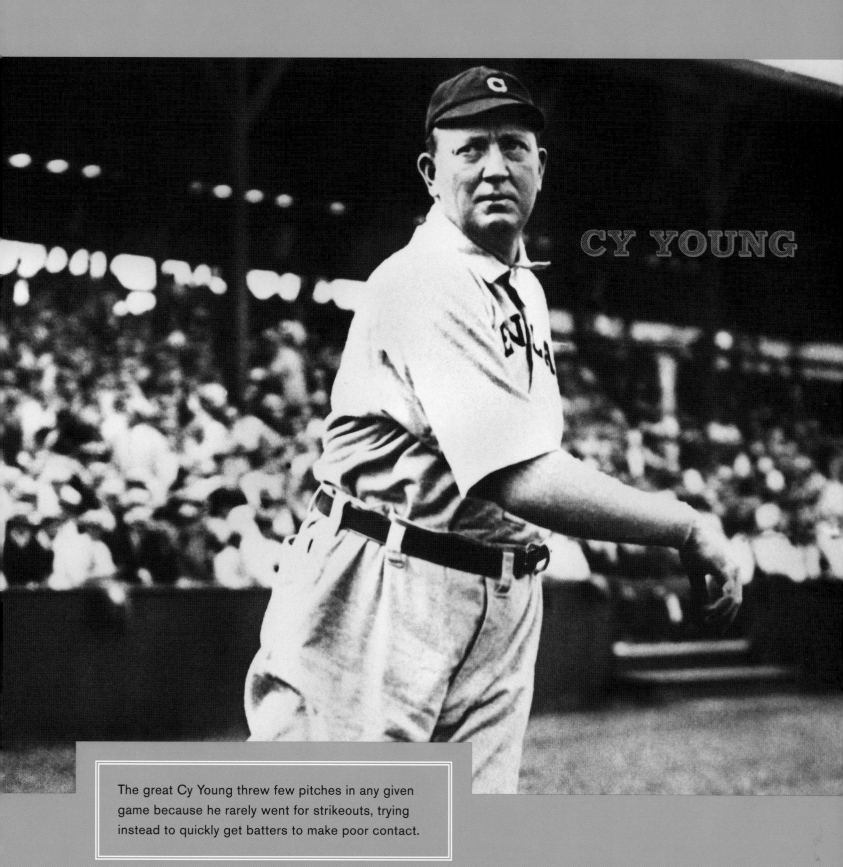

CY YOUNG

The great Cy Young threw few pitches in any given game because he rarely went for strikeouts, trying instead to quickly get batters to make poor contact.

THE GREATEST BATTING RACE

One of the most intriguing stories of baseball's 1910 season was the batting race between Indians second baseman Nap Lajoie and Detroit Tigers outfielder Ty Cobb. In 1910, Lajoie smacked the ball to every corner of the park, hitting well above .350 for most of the year. As the season wound down, he and Cobb were locked in a race for the AL batting title. To add some flavor to the contest, the Chalmers Automobile Company promised a brand-new car to the winner. Cobb, believing that he had first place in the bag, sat out his final two games to preserve his average. Lajoie, on the last day of the regular season, played in a doubleheader against the St. Louis Browns and got hits in eight of his nine at bats, bunting seven of those. The next day, some papers proclaimed Lajoie the winner, while others crowned Cobb. *The Sporting News* stated that Cobb had won, beating Lajoie .384944 to .384084, but the Chalmers Company was not as decisive; in the end, it gave both players a car. Ninety years later, it was determined that Cobb mistakenly got credit for two extra hits, but Major League Baseball refused to change the official record.

CATCHER · SANDY ALOMAR JR.

In his first season with the Indians in 1990, Sandy Alomar was named a Gold Glove winner, an All-Star, and only the third unanimous Rookie of the Year choice in AL history. Seven years later, Alomar assembled a midseason 30-game hitting streak that fell just 1 game short of second baseman Nap Lajoie's club record, set in 1906. He also helped lead the Indians to a World Series appearance that year, hitting .367 with two home runs in the series. Sandy was the son of former California Angels All-Star second baseman Sandy Alomar Sr. and brother to big-league second baseman Roberto Alomar, a 12-time All-Star.

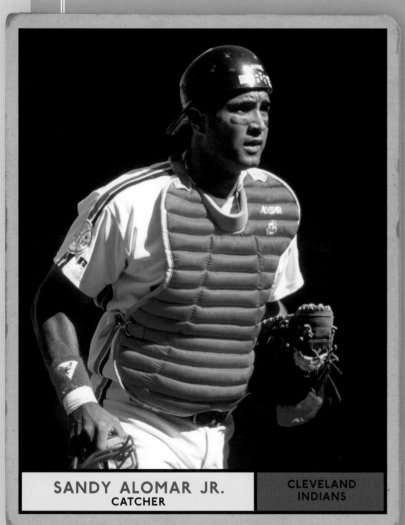

SANDY ALOMAR JR.
CATCHER

CLEVELAND
INDIANS

STATS

Indians seasons: 1990–2000

Height: 6-foot-5

Weight: 235

• 1,236 career hits

• .311 World Series BA

• 1990 AL Rookie of the Year

• 6-time All-Star

FIRST BASEMAN · JIM THOME

Before Cleveland drafted him in 1989, Jim Thome grew up a Chicago Cubs fan in Peoria, Illinois, and was a two-sport star in baseball and basketball throughout high school and college. Thome hit his stride in 1995, when he bashed 25 home runs and batted .314. But that was only the beginning; in 1996, he hit 38 home runs. He just kept slugging away, hitting 49 in 2001 and 52 (a career high) in 2002. Because Thome's hitting success also translated into financial success, he was able to put all 10 of his nieces and nephews through college.

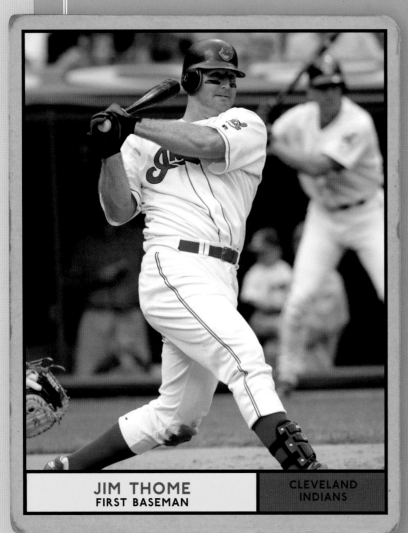

JIM THOME
FIRST BASEMAN

CLEVELAND
INDIANS

STATS

Indians seasons: 1991–2002

Height: 6-foot-4

Weight: 220

• 1,624 career RBI

• 589 career HR

• 2003 AL leader in HR (47)

• 5-time All-Star

NAP'S CHAPS

y 1908, Lajoie had the Naps battling the Detroit Tigers for first place in the AL. The race was a close one, but in the end, the Naps fell a half-game short of the pennant. Joss had greater individual success; on October 2, he threw a perfect game against the Chicago White Sox, retiring all 27 batters in a row. "Joss sort of hid the ball on you," said St. Louis Browns shortstop Bobby Wallace. "One moment you'd be squinting at a long graceful windup, and the next instant, out of nowhere, the ball was hopping across the plate."

The Naps brought Cy Young back to Cleveland in 1909. When legendary left fielder "Shoeless Joe" Jackson came on board the following season, the Naps seemed ready to contend again. But even the powerful bats of Lajoie and Jackson couldn't make up for what happened next. The team suffered two big losses in 1911 when Young left town and the 31-year-old Joss died suddenly of a bacterial disease called tubercular meningitis. The team continued to slide in the AL standings until 1914, when it finished in last place and parted ways with Lajoie.

After Nap's departure, the team was renamed the Indians, but the name change did nothing to improve the club's performance on the field. It wasn't until the Indians traded for center fielder Tris Speaker in 1916 that they began to see positive results. The fleet-footed Speaker played so close to second base that he was more like a fifth infielder, yet his speed still let him run down most deep shots. "Tris played the shallowest center field I've seen," said Cleveland sportswriter Hal Lebovitz. "I seldom saw anyone hit the ball over his head."

Halfway through the 1919 season, Speaker was named player/manager and led the team to a second-place finish. Expectations were high for an even better year in 1920, but tragedy struck on August 16, when talented shortstop Ray Chapman was killed after taking a pitch to the head. Surprisingly, the downhearted "Tribe" rallied to win 24 of its last 32 games, capturing its first AL pennant. Cleveland faced the Brooklyn Dodgers in the World Series, and after four games, the teams were tied two games to two. In Game 5, the Indians claimed the upper hand, winning 8–1. They didn't allow a single run in the next two games, winning both to capture their first world championship.

The rest of the 1920s featured fine efforts from such players as shortstop Joe Sewell, but the Indians never seriously contended for

TRIS SPEAKER

Tris Speaker combined speed, smarts, and a keen batting eye. One of his favorite tactics in the field was to sneak up to second base and receive a throw from the catcher in an attempt to pick off an unwary base runner.

SECOND BASEMAN · NAP LAJOIE

Known for his easy smile and jokester personality, Nap Lajoie was well-liked by both teammates and opponents. Even though his batting stance appeared somewhat lazy, Lajoie worked tirelessly to become one of the best hitters in baseball. He hit over .300 in 16 of his 21 years in the big leagues and was such an incredible all-around player that Cleveland named the team after him for a while (1903–14). He led the league four times in hits and doubles, and so formidable was his reputation that, in a 1901 game, he became the first player ever to be intentionally walked with the bases loaded.

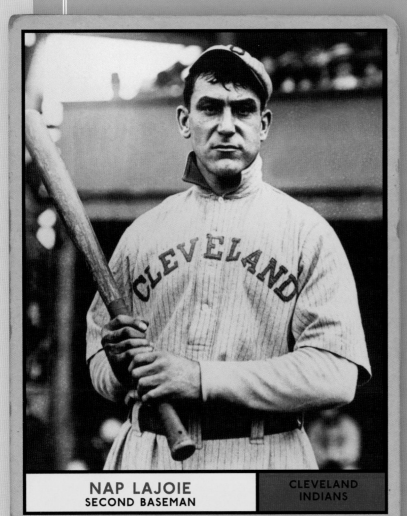

NAP LAJOIE
SECOND BASEMAN

CLEVELAND
INDIANS

STATS

Indians seasons: 1902–14

Height: 6-foot-1

Weight: 195

- **1,599 career RBI**

- **.338 career BA**

- **1901 AL Triple Crown winner (leader in BA, HR, and RBI)**

- **Baseball Hall of Fame inductee (1937)**

the pennant. On July 31, 1932, an overflow crowd of 80,000 turned out to welcome the Indians to their new home, the 78,000-seat Municipal Stadium. "When I went to the mound and looked around at the crowd, it was the most awesome thing I'd ever seen," recalled hurler Mel Harder. "I mean, 80,000 fans. It was hard to believe so many people could be in one place." Unfortunately, the park wasn't fan-friendly—especially when clouds of mosquitoes moved from the shores of Lake Erie and onto spectators. Municipal Stadium soon became a ghost town, and the Indians reverted to playing day games at their former home, League Park.

Fans had something to take their minds off the stadium woes when Cleveland signed 17-year-old pitcher Bob Feller in 1936. "Rapid Robert" would live up to his nickname, leading the AL in strikeouts seven times, thanks to a sizzling fastball that became the stuff of legend. Even famed Chicago White Sox pitcher Ted Lyons could hardly believe the speed of Feller's "heater," saying, "It wasn't until you hit against him that you knew how fast he really was, until you saw with your own eyes that ball jumping at you."

Four years later, Rapid Robert was hitting his peak. On opening day of the 1940 season, Feller threw a no-hitter against the White Sox, and the Indians played tug-of-war with the Tigers for the pennant all year.

STAN COVELESKI

WORLD SERIES FIRSTS

In 1920, the Indians—led by star outfielder Tris Speaker—were tops in the AL in doubles, runs batted in (RBI), walks, and runs scored. Not only that, but pitcher Jim Bagby led the league in wins, and Stan Coveleski boasted the most strikeouts. This loaded team faced the Brooklyn Dodgers in a best-of-nine World Series in October 1920. The Indians beat the Dodgers five games to two, with Coveleski winning three of those games. But most notable was the fifth game of the series. In the first inning, with the bases loaded, Indians outfielder Elmer Smith hit a grand slam (the first ever in World Series history). In the fourth, with two men on base, Bagby smacked a home run, becoming the first pitcher ever to hit a home run in a World Series. Then, in the fifth inning, with runners on first and second, Cleveland second baseman Bill Wambsganss caught a fly ball, stepped on the base to put out Dodgers second baseman Pete Kilduff, then tagged out catcher Otto Miller, who was running from first. It was the first—and still the only—unassisted triple play in the history of the "Fall Classic."

After having a five-and-a-half-game lead evaporate in early September, the team stumbled through the next few weeks to finish one game behind the Tigers. When the U.S. entered World War II the next year, many baseball players, including Feller, went off to fight, stranding the Indians at the bottom of the AL.

THE BILL VEECK ERA

By the time the war ended in 1945, shortstop Lou Boudreau had become player/manager of the Indians. In 1946, Feller was back from the conflict and to top form, winning 26 games with a club-record 348 strikeouts. "I didn't know much," Feller later said humbly about his pitching strategies. "I just reared back and let them go. Where the ball went was up to heaven."

New owner Bill Veeck made sure, though, that Feller was not the only attraction at Indians games. Cleveland finished in sixth place in 1946, but attendance topped one million for the first time, due to Veeck's attention-grabbing antics. He gave out prizes, shot off fireworks, and

THIRD BASEMAN · AL ROSEN

A former amateur boxer who broke his nose 11 times, Al Rosen spent his entire 10-year career with the Indians. In his first full season (1950), he hit a league-leading 37 home runs, which was an AL record for rookies at the time. In 1953, he hit 43 homers and posted 145 RBI but was one hit shy of having the AL's best batting average, narrowly missing the Triple Crown. After he retired from baseball at the relatively young age of 32, he went on to become a stockbroker and then the general manager of three major-league teams.

STATS

AL ROSEN
THIRD BASEMAN

CLEVELAND INDIANS

Indians seasons: 1947–56

Height: 5-foot-10

Weight: 180

• 1953 AL MVP

• 4-time All-Star

• 5 seasons of 100-plus RBI

• 2-time AL leader in HR

Red Sox great Ted Williams called Bob Lemon "one of the very best pitchers I ever faced. His ball was always moving, hard, sinking, fast-breaking."

drove relief pitchers to the mound in a red jeep, among other things. Veeck continued his groundbreaking moves in 1947 by signing the first African American ever to play in the AL, center fielder Larry Doby, who would become a seven-time All-Star.

The next year, Bob Lemon, a sinkerball specialist, racked up 20 wins and helped the Indians squeak by the Boston Red Sox to claim the AL pennant. The Tribe faced the Boston Braves in a 1948 World Series that was all about pitching. In Game 1, Feller threw a two-hit gem, but the Indians struggled at the plate and lost. Cleveland won the next three games, but Game 5 found the Indians trailing in the late innings, so Boudreau sent hurler Satchel Paige in to see what he could accomplish. Paige, fresh from the Negro Leagues, then became the first African American to pitch in a World Series. Unfortunately, his two-thirds of an inning was not impressive, and he was quickly replaced. The Indians

BOB LEMON

ended up getting drubbed 11–5, but they would not be denied their ultimate victory. Cleveland won 4–3 in Game 6 to claim its first world championship since 1920.

Cleveland could not parlay that title into success the following season, though. The Indians' dive to third place prompted Veeck to sell the club, and in 1951, Boudreau was replaced as manager. In 1953, slugging third baseman Al Rosen won the AL Most Valuable Player (MVP) award, and in 1954, when the Tribe won a league-record 111 games, Indians fans were confident that their team would prove invincible as it faced the New York Giants in the World Series. Game 1 was a nail-biter, going to the bottom of the 10th inning before the Giants squeezed out a 5–2 victory. The stunned Indians never recovered, and the Giants went on to sweep all four games. Cleveland fans hoped for another shot at the title the next year, but the Indians fell short of the pennant. In fact, 41 years would pass before the Indians would make it back to postseason play.

A BANNER YEAR

The 1953 season ended in frustration in Cleveland, as the Indians finished second to the Yankees for the third year in a row. There was no indication that 1954 was going to be any different when the Indians kept pace with the "Bronx Bombers" early on. Then, starting on May 13, the Tribe went on an 11-game winning streak and, by June, reached first place. In June and July, the Indians won 41 games, but the Yankees were hot on their trail, winning 43 of their own. New York stayed close until September, when the teams met for a doubleheader in Cleveland's Municipal Stadium. A record 84,587 fans turned out to see if the Indians could finally put their archenemy away. In the first game, Indians hurler Bob Lemon threw a six-hitter to win. The next game, pitcher Early Wynn outdid Lemon, throwing a three-hitter to beat the Yankees. In the end, the Indians closed the season with a league-record 111 wins, leaving the Yankees a full 8 games behind. Although they eventually lost the World Series to the New York Giants, 1954 went down as a banner year for the Indians.

INDIANS

SHORTSTOP · OMAR VIZQUEL

For more than 20 years, Omar Vizquel used his ability to seamlessly turn double plays and catch ground balls barehanded to put out frustrated batters. He once tied a big-league record set by Baltimore Orioles great Cal Ripken Jr. by going an amazing 95 games without committing a single error. In 2002, he made only 7 errors in 150 games, yet the Gold Glove award for outstanding defense went to another shortstop, the Texas Rangers' Alex Rodriguez. Vizquel was the perfect number-two batter, an unselfish switch hitter who, in 2004, led the AL with 20 sacrifice bunts.

OMAR VIZQUEL
SHORTSTOP

CLEVELAND
INDIANS

STATS

Indians seasons: 1994–2004

Height: 5-foot-9

Weight: 175

- .273 career BA

- .985 career fielding percentage

- 3-time All-Star

- 11-time Gold Glove winner

THE CURSE OF ROCKY COLAVITO

Right fielder Rocky Colavito joined the Indians in 1955. The 6-foot-3 kid from the Bronx, New York, belted more than 40 home runs in both 1958 and 1959, becoming the first Indians player to achieve such a feat. Colavito became an instant hometown favorite not only for his bat but also for the marathon autograph sessions he held after each game.

With Colavito's popularity on the rise, 1960 seemed full of promise for the Indians. But before the season started, general manager Frank "Trader" Lane made an unlucky and hugely unpopular deal in trading the beloved Colavito to the Tigers. The Indians dropped to fourth place that year and would take more than 30 years to recover from what some called the "Curse of Rocky Colavito."

Throughout the 1960s and '70s, the Tribe seemed to keep giving away their best players for little in return—

ROCKY COLAVITO

LEFT FIELDER · JOE JACKSON

Before arriving in Cleveland, Joe Jackson was a South Carolina mill worker who couldn't read or write. But he could play baseball. While working at the mill, Jackson had acquired the nickname "Shoeless Joe" for playing a game in his socks because a new pair of shoes had given him blisters the day before. In his first full season with the Cleveland Naps, the hardworking rookie hit .408. For his involvement in the infamous Chicago "Black Sox" gambling scandal of the 1919 World Series, Jackson was banned for life from professional ball, but he continued to play in semipro leagues throughout the South for many years.

JOE JACKSON
LEFT FIELDER

CLEVELAND INDIANS

STATS

Indians seasons: 1910–15

Height: 6-foot-1

Weight: 200

- **3-time AL leader in triples**
- **.356 career BA**
- **.345 career World Series BA**
- **785 career RBI**

HOME SWEET HOME

Over the past 100 years, the Cleveland Indians have called three unique ballparks home. The first, League Park, was built in 1891 and eventually had a capacity of 20,000. Because the field had to fit into a cramped city grid, it had some unusual dimensions. The right-field line was only 290 feet from home plate, but for players to hit a home run, the ball had to get over a 60-foot wall—that's 23 feet taller than Boston's famous "Green Monster" in Fenway Park! The second field, Municipal Stadium, opened in 1931 and could house up to 78,000. It was dubbed "The Mistake by the Lake" by fans because of its size and the strong winds that blew in off Lake Erie. The center-field stands were 480 feet from home plate, and no player ever hit a home run that far. Indians owner Bill Veeck sometimes moved Municipal's outfield fence 15 feet in or out, depending on how it would favor his team. The team's third home, Jacobs Field, opened in 1994 at about half the size of old Municipal Stadium, but it featured the largest freestanding scoreboard in the United States and one of the largest video screens in the world.

INDIANS

except in the case of star pitcher Sam McDowell, who reigned as the AL strikeout king in five of the six seasons from 1965 to 1970. In 1965, "Sudden Sam" struck out 325 batters and posted an earned run average (ERA) of 2.18. He won a career-best 20 games in 1970, but the Indians fell into a slump and traded him a year later for future Cy Young Award winner Gaylord Perry. Perry's illegal spitballs were notorious—but generally overlooked by umpires—and he threw them often to win 24 games in 1972.

The rest of the '70s and '80s were lean baseball years in Cleveland. Throughout both decades, the Tribe would finish no better than fourth place in the AL Eastern Division (the league had been split into two divisions in 1969). Although highlights were few and far between, two pitchers made positive headlines. Dennis Eckersley, who would later find his true niche as the closer for the Oakland A's and eventually be enshrined in the Hall of Fame, threw a no-hitter as a starter in 1977, the last of his three seasons with the Indians. In 1981, Lenny Barker had a day to remember, throwing a perfect game versus the Toronto Blue Jays at Municipal Stadium.

In 1994, the Indians moved into a new stadium, Jacobs Field, and a new division, the AL Central. That season was cut short

GAYLORD PERRY

The defense of Omar Vizquel (left) and slugging of Albert Belle (right) helped transform the Indians from doormat to contender in the mid-1990s.

by a players' strike that wiped out the second half of the schedule, but after the strike finally ended in 1995, the Tribe emerged as an AL power again. That year, the Indians fought their way to the best record in the league and won the AL Central by an incredible 30 games. Big catcher Sandy Alomar Jr. and sure-gloved shortstop Omar Vizquel led Cleveland's defense, and burly designated hitter Albert Belle led the offense, becoming the first player in major-league history to hit more than 50 home runs and 50 doubles in a season. Speedy center fielder Kenny Lofton, meanwhile, led the league in stolen bases for the fourth year in a row.

The Tribe swept the Boston Red Sox in the first round of the playoffs. Then they battled the Seattle Mariners in the AL Championship Series (ALCS), winning the series four games to two. After 41 years, the Indians were finally back in the World Series, this time opposite the Atlanta Braves. The series was a tight affair, with five of the six games decided by a single run. In the end, though, Atlanta's superior pitching prevailed, and the Indians went home empty-handed.

Cleveland's baseball passion only increased the next year, as tickets for the entire 1996 season sold out before opening day. The Indians didn't disappoint their excited fan base, storming to 99 victories to again post the best record in the AL. But in the AL Division Series (ALDS), Cleveland was eliminated by the Baltimore Orioles in four games.

To make another run at the pennant in 1997, the Indians decided to get another power hitter, trading Lofton for slugging outfielder David Justice. The swap paid off. Justice hit .329 and bashed 33 dingers that year to help Cleveland win the AL Central again. The Indians then beat the Yankees and Orioles in the playoffs to make their second World Series appearance in three years.

The Indians faced the five-year-old Florida Marlins in what turned out to be one of the most dramatic World Series in years. After six

CENTER FIELDER · TRIS SPEAKER

The second player ever to win the AL MVP award (after Detroit Tigers great Ty Cobb), Tris Speaker proved time and again that he was one of the greatest center fielders of his day. His unique style of playing a shallow center field allowed him to make 436 outfield assists and to turn 139 double plays throughout his career. He led the league 8 times in hitting doubles, and he assembled 3 hitting streaks of 20 or more games in a single season (1912). Named player/manager in 1919, Speaker led the Indians to a World Series title in 1920.

TRIS SPEAKER
CENTER FIELDER

CLEVELAND
INDIANS

STATS

Indians seasons: 1916–26

Height: 5-foot-11

Weight: 193

- **1,882 career runs scored**

- **.345 career BA**

- **792 career doubles (most all-time)**

- **Baseball Hall of Fame inductee (1937)**

games, the series was tied three games to three, and everything came down to Game 7, which went into extra innings. In the bottom of the 11th, Marlins shortstop Edgar Renteria drove in the winning run, crushing Cleveland's hopes for its first World Series championship since 1948. "About a year and a half or so after that World Series," Indians manager Mike Hargrove later said, "a guy asked me how long it took me to get over that last game. I told him, 'As soon as it happens, I'll let you know.'"

THE TRIBE REGROUPS

Despite that bitter loss, the Indians were ready for another go in 1998. They reacquired Kenny Lofton and again captured the division, topping the Red Sox in the ALDS and then meeting the Yankees in the ALCS. Cleveland came up short, four games to two, and had to take consolation in being the only team that year to win any postseason games against the eventual world champion Yankees, who reigned as the most powerful team in the major leagues in the late 1990s.

Power-hitting right fielder Manny Ramirez carried much of Cleveland's offensive load in 1999, setting a club record with a whopping 165 RBI. "Manny does everything so effortlessly, and the ball just jumps off his bat," said Hargrove. "He has the talent to hit a pitch no matter where the pitcher throws it." The Indians posted a 97–65 record that season, becoming just the third team in major-league history to win five consecutive division titles. But it didn't matter in the end; the Red Sox topped the Indians in the first round of the playoffs.

WELCOME TO CLEVELAND STADIUM

SILVER-SCREEN SLUGGERS

The 1989 movie *Major League* offered a fictional account of the Cleveland Indians. In the film, the Indians are bought by a money-hungry owner who wants to move the team to Florida and therefore tries to drive fan support down by throwing together a roster full of losers and has-beens. But, predictably yet comically, the misfits come together to find success and save both the season and the franchise for Cleveland. Although Cleveland fans knew they were just watching actors wearing replica Indians uniforms, the movie's story of a sad-sack team and a fan base with low expectations hit very close to home, since the real-life Indians hadn't been truly competitive since the 1950s. Starring Charlie Sheen as Rickie "Wild Thing" Vaughn, a heartthrob relief pitcher with control problems; Wesley Snipes as Willie Mays Hayes, a super-fast base stealer who can't get on base; and Tom Berenger as Jake Taylor, an aging catcher with rickety knees, the movie (which received an R rating due to adult language) was a surprise hit with moviegoers. *New York Times* movie reviewer Caryn James wrote, "*Major League* trots out the standard formula but has the wit to make fun of it now and then."

RIGHT FIELDER · MANNY RAMIREZ

Originally from Santo Domingo, the Dominican Republic, Ramirez spent his teenage years in New York City. Widely regarded as one of the most versatile hitters in the league, the powerful outfielder with the laid-back personality hit against right-handed and left-handed pitchers with equal success. During his Indians career, he rang up 236 home runs and 804 RBI. He posted a career-best 165 RBI in 1999. That total was not only the highest in the majors since 1938, but it made him the first player since Red Sox great Ted Williams in 1949 to have more RBI in a season than games played. In 2001, he left Cleveland for Boston.

MANNY RAMIREZ
RIGHT FIELDER

CLEVELAND
INDIANS

STATS

Indians seasons: 1993–2000

Height: 6 feet

Weight: 200

- 555 career HR

- 1,830 career RBI

- 2004 World Series MVP

- 12-time All-Star

MANAGER · LOU BOUDREAU

At age 24, Boudreau became the youngest player ever to manage a major-league team for an entire season. In his first six years, his inexperience showed, as the Tribe never placed higher than third. Club owners weren't impressed. In 1945, they tried to replace him, but Cleveland fans protested so much that the Indians kept him on. It was a good thing they did; a few years later, he led the Indians to a World Series title. Before becoming their manager, Boudreau was an excellent shortstop for the Indians and one of the AL's top fielders in the 1940s.

STATS

**Indians seasons as manager:
1942–50**

Managerial record: 1,162–1,224

World Series championship: 1948

**Baseball Hall of Fame inductee
(1970)**

LOU BOUDREAU
MANAGER

CLEVELAND
INDIANS

The Indians allowed Ramirez to join the Red Sox as a free agent in 2001, but strapping first baseman Jim Thome took up the slack, clubbing 49 home runs—the most in team history for a left-handed hitter. Young southpaw pitcher C. C. Sabathia won a club-high 17 games, and the Indians went 91–71 to earn another postseason berth. This time they were sent home by the Seattle Mariners.

Cleveland slid from the ranks of the contenders in 2002, finishing below .500 for the first time in nine campaigns. Team management made a change in 2003, hiring Eric Wedge as Cleveland's new skipper, but the Indians remained an inconsistent club over the next few seasons, sandwiching losing records around an impressive 93–69 campaign in 2005.

In 2007, though, the Indians finally returned to the form they had shown throughout the late '90s. The stars aligned for the Tribe's pitching staff when Sabathia and fellow starter Fausto Carmona turned in sterling seasons, each notching 19 victories, and closer Joe Borowski

C. C. SABATHIA

posted an AL-best 45 saves. Cleveland's lineup, meanwhile, was packed with players who hit for both average and power, including switch-hitting catcher Victor Martinez, swift center fielder Grady Sizemore, and burly designated hitter Travis Hafner.

The 2007 Indians ran away with the AL Central, finishing 96–66, and then mowed down the Yankees in the ALDS. In the ALCS, Cleveland met Boston and staked a three-games-to-one lead. Unfortunately, the Tribe then collapsed, losing the next three games—by a combined score of 30–5—to finish one win shy of the World Series. "This is the greatest group of guys I've ever been a part of," said pitcher Paul Byrd, who won each of his two postseason starts. "The way this team played, the way this team hustled, the way this team fought against adversity was just an absolute pleasure and an absolute blast to watch."

The 2008 Indians seemed primed for another World Series run, but injuries to key stars and disappointing performances from other players left Cleveland a middling 81–81. The main bright spot was veteran pitcher Cliff Lee, who went 22–3 to capture the AL Cy Young Award. Sadly, Cleveland's slide continued in 2009, as Lee was traded away in midseason, and the Indians finished fourth in the AL Central

CONTENDERS ONCE AGAIN

In 1995, after Major League Baseball's players' strike was over, the Indians put together one of their most impressive seasons ever, winning their first AL pennant since 1954. Indians pitchers led the league with the lowest team ERA (3.83), and outfielder Albert Belle became the first major-leaguer to collect 100 extra-base hits since 1948. In the divisional playoffs against the Red Sox, the first game was not decided until the bottom of the 13th inning, when Indians catcher Tony Peña slammed a home run and gave the Tribe a shot of momentum. They took the rest of the series and went on to beat the Seattle Mariners in the ALCS, propelling them into the World Series. In the first two games against the Atlanta Braves in the Fall Classic, the Indians lost by one run. Game 3 was at home in Jacobs Field, and designated hitter Eddie Murray slapped a game-winning single to give Cleveland its first win in a World Series game in 47 years. Although the Indians eventually lost the World Series, just being there was an accomplishment for a team that had suffered one of the longest playoff droughts in league history.

INDIANS

GRADY SIZEMORE

At 6-foot-2 and 200 pounds, Grady Sizemore was a rare blend of power and speed, slamming 33 homers and swiping 38 bags in 2008.

SHIN-SOO CHOO

The steady hitting of Shin-Soo Choo (opposite) and pitching efforts of Mitch Talbot (below) were bright spots during Cleveland's otherwise lackluster 2010 season.

that season and the next. Right fielder Shin-Soo Choo batted .300 in 2010 under new manager Manny Acta, but the Indians went just 69–93.

As home to the Forest Citys, the Spiders, and the Indians, Cleveland has a rich major-league history that goes back more than 140 years. And although their beloved Tribe has not hoisted a World Series trophy since 1948, Cleveland fans refuse to be soured by the drought. For they know that when their Indians do claim that long-awaited third world championship, the victory will be all the sweeter.

MITCH TALBOT

INDIANS

INDEX